John Bhaid.

13-10-47

BRITAIN IN PICTURES
THE BRITISH PEOPLE IN PICTURES

BRITISH PHILOSOPHERS

GENERAL EDITOR

W. J. TURNER

The Editor is most grateful to all those who have
so kindly helped in the selection of illustrations,
especially to officials of the various public
Museums, Libraries and Galleries, and
to all others who have generously
allowed pictures and MSS.
to be reproduced

BRITISH PHILOSOPHERS

KENNETH MATTHEWS

WITH
8 PLATES IN COLOUR
AND
14 ILLUSTRATIONS IN
BLACK & WHITE

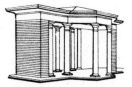

WILLIAM COLLINS OF LONDON
MCMXXXXIII

PRODUCED BY
ADPRINT LIMITED LONDON

PRINTED
IN GREAT BRITAIN BY
WM. COLLINS SONS AND CO. LTD. GLASGOW
ON MELLOTEX BOOK PAPER
MADE BY TULLIS RUSSELL & CO. LTD.
MARKINCH FIFE

LIST OF ILLUSTRATIONS

PLATES IN COLOUR

BLACK AND WHITE ILUSTRATIONS

DUKE HUMPHREY'S LIBRARY, THE BODLEIAN
Engraving by David Loggan, 1675

I

TWO major influences have shaped the philosophy of modern Europe: the British and the German. It is true that Descartes, who is generally regarded as the founder of modern European philosophy, was a Frenchman and Spinoza, the saintly, Ghandi-like refugee who polished lenses and discoursed with princes, was a Spanish Jew. No science can be confined behind national frontiers. But just as in Ancient Greece an extraordinary coruscation of intellectual curiosity took place in a brief period and within the limits of a single language, so in Britain a tradition of philosophy arose and flourished, having its special native characteristics ; and so in Germany a rival succession of philosophers flourished in their turn, following different gods.

The native characteristics of British philosophy are these: common sense, dislike of complication, a strong preference for the concrete over the abstract and a certain awkward honesty of method in which an occasional pearl of poetry is embedded. It is as easy to perceive a common parentage in the philosophies of John Locke and Bertrand Russell as in the seamanship of Francis Drake and Horatio Nelson. We might vainly enquire whether climate or language or some original hereditary strain or a combination of all three produces the distinguishing marks of national character, but their existence cannot be denied. The British philosophers, at least the most typical of them, stand with both feet on the ground. They are, compared with the great German system builders, Kant, Hegel, Leibniz and the others, earthbound and pedestrian figures. But then, they would say, a sound philosophy is a utility product, which must be capable of taking hard knocks.

A crucial incident in the history of European philosophy was the discovery of David Hume by Immanuel Kant. The German philosopher tells us in a memorable phrase that he was suddenly "awakened from his dogmatic slumbers." We do not know which of Hume's books provoked this event, nor exactly when it happened. It was probably one of the passages in the *Treatise of Human Nature*, one of those destructive analyses of the idea of causation, which struck Kant as somehow darkly anarchic and led him to create the elaborate philosophic structure of the *Critique of Pure Reason*. It would be too much to attribute all the ambitious philosophic systems which were evolved by German philosophers after Kant to the seed sown in Kant's mind by the Scottish philosopher. There are fashions in philosophy, as in everything else ; and in the Romantic Period, people were ready for philosophies in the romantic spirit and on a romantic scale. The fellow-countrymen of Wagner supplied them. They had their influence in the world ; and they had their imitators in Britain. But when a philosophy erected like Kant's or Hegel's, tier upon tier of abstract superstructure upon a pinpoint of experience, falls out of fashion, it falls like Lucifer, never to rise again. The philosophy which touches the ground at many points has a much greater survival value.

Moreover, common sense is not a dull quality. Rather the contrary. Nothing is more calculated to shock people than common sense applied to long established but unexamined beliefs. This was the indiscretion which long ago put a cup of hemlock in front of Socrates.

The British philosophers provoked the same reactions, but on the whole did not go to the same lengths of contumacy Sir Thomas More was the only one to lose his life and that for annoying the King rather than writing *Utopia*. Thomas Hobbes, the truculent author of *Leviathan*, went more often to church when a Bill denouncing his famous work as blasphemous literature was introduced in Parliament. Locke went into exile, as Socrates might have done ; his *Letter on Toleration* was published in Holland. Hume, than whom no man lived a more blameless life, ensconced in his Edinburgh house, with his sister, maid and cat, was regarded with such distrust that hostile demonstrations were expected at his funeral ; and on the advice of his friends, he kept the *Dialogues Concerning Natural Religion* unpublished during his lifetime. Undoubtedly a certain mellowing in the public attitude towards philosophic speculation was taking place even at that time ; philosophers, like heretics and witches, had succeeded in somewhat modifying their professional status. But it was still possible for Jeremy Bentham to horrify the Romantic Age by the classical simplicity of the Utilitarian doctrine : the greatest happiness of the greatest number. John Stuart Mill tells us how he read Bentham in his teens with an effect of revelation ; and no doubt (though this is not recorded) there were murmurings in conservative households that Mr. Bentham must have picked up these immoral ideas during his travels in Russia.

Bentham journeyed to Russia and wrote one of his books in the form of letters from Russia. We have noted the practical spirit of British

NORTH VIEW OF FRIAR BACON'S STUDY AT OXFORD
Coloured aquatint by T. Rowlandson, 1756-1827

Johannes Duns Scotus, Doctor - Subtilis

DUNS SCOTUS
17th Century oil painting

philosophy ; and it should not surprise us to find that the philosophers themselves were practical men. Men of affairs would be an even juster description. Two of them, Francis Bacon and Thomas More, occupied the office of Lord Chancellor ; hence Harvey's celebrated taunt, that Bacon wrote philosophy like a Lord Chancellor. Locke was offered the post of Ambassador at Vienna or Berlin ; and actually filled the offices of Secretary to the Board of Trade, Commissioner of Appeals and Commissioner of Trade and Plantations. Berkeley spent ten years of his life on a plan for a college in the Bermudas, whose purpose would be "the reformation of manners among the English in our Western plantations and the propagation of the Gospel among the American savages" ; and if the project never matured, it must be recorded that a grant of money was made by the almost unanimous vote of the House of Commons. Bentham was one of the pioneers of British prison reform. J. S. Mill was for twenty years in charge of the East India Company's relations with the Indian native states. Those philosophers who, like Hume, had none but literary ambitions, regarded philosophy not as an end in itself, but as a foundation of other researches ; they concerned themselves with history, social problems, economics and theories of government. We may conclude either that the common sense which we have mentioned as a characteristic of British philosophers derives from this catholic experience, or that both philosophy and experience derive from an innate realism of mind.

What is Philosophy ? The old Greek word meant simply "love of wisdom." In the popular sense, philosophy means any deeply reflective study of abstract subjects, like God or Beauty. In this sense the poets are philosophers ; and Browning and Wordsworth are more philosophic than Herrick or Keats. This opinion seems to me to be true as far as it goes.

But in a narrow sense philosophy means what Aristotle first called metaphysics. By metaphysics we understand the science which supplies the answer to the question : what is the nature of the universe ; or to break up the subject into its component terms, what is space, what is time, what is the mind of man made of, what is the difference between mind and matter, what do we mean when we say that a thing exists, and so on. Closely associated with metaphysics, we have ethics, which purports to answer the question : what is the Good and how ought man to behave ; and logic, which is the formal analysis of our methods of reasoning. It is clear that no exact dividing line exists enclosing philosophy on one side and non-philosophy on the other. There is rather a progress from questions which are felt to be absolutely fundamental and secondary questions which arise therefrom. Like most living things, philosophy does not easily submit to academic definitions. But it will probably be most useful if we think of philosophy mainly in the narrow metaphysical sense but without altogether excluding the more generous interpretations.

9

II

SOME of the most remarkable relics in England are the churches and monasteries surviving among the Northumbrian shipyards from the days of the Venerable Bede. We shall not claim Bede as a philosopher, although he died like one, surrounded by weeping disciples and dictating the last words of his English translation of the Gospel of St. John.

Small, isolated communities like Bede's kept a candle burning in Britain during the early Middle Ages. But the centres of learning were on the Continent of Europe : the Frankish Courts, the Vatican, the University of Paris. Charlemagne wanted to see the intellectual life of Europe revolving round his own person ; while he exchanged gifts with the Caliph of the Arabian world, he called scholars from south, north, east and west, including Alcuin from Britain. We shall not call Alcuin a philosopher ; nor yet Erigena, who travelled from Ireland to the Court of Charles the Bald. Both were theologians, for whom philosophy was one of God's handmaids, subject both to divine discipline and original sin. All through the Middle Ages you were allowed to philosophise only if your conclusions served to buttress the current dogmas of the Church ; Aristotle, read in Latin translations, was the "set book." The story of British philosophy is the story of how this ghostly tyranny was broken, how independent thought on fundamental questions was achieved and what it accomplished.

We might do worse than begin with the Franciscan mission which landed at Dover on September 10th, 1224, not for the mission's own sake but because of its connection with Britain's first full-size philosopher, Roger Bacon. What strange invasions the coast of Kent has seen—the legions of Julius Caesar, the war-craft of the Anglo-Saxons, St. Augustine's little Christian band, and, on this old September Tuesday, the nine friars sent by St. Francis, three of them Englishmen, who journeyed to Lincoln, London and Oxford to set up new standards of scholarship in England. The Franciscan School in Oxford was of especial importance ; there an infant university was arising which was soon to rival Paris, and the Franciscans played a great part in its development. We are told how the friars used to walk barefoot through the cold and wind to attend the Oxford theology classes. They quickly produced philosophers pre-eminent in their generation : Thomas of York, whose *Metaphysics* was preserved in Italian libraries in Florence and the Vatican ; Friar Robert of Cornwall "whom the fools thought wise and wise men crazy" in Roger Bacon's biting phrase (he was rash enough to differ from Bacon on a point of logic !) ; and Stephen the Englishman who lectured on philosophy in Genoa and Rome and who, when dying, besought his friend to have masses said for his soul "because he used to go too often to a certain religious matron, to console her."

'The Philosophers on the Summit of Mount Athos taking Observations of the Stars and writing Words in the Dust'
Illumination from the Travels of Sir John Mandeville. 15th century

Roger Bacon (Friar Bacon) joined the Franciscan Order in Paris ; between Paris and Oxford he divided his life. A prodigious figure ! He has survived in legend as the inventor of gunpowder. Popular opinion is at least right in judging him to be the sort of person who might have made this discovery. Popular opinion has also dressed him in a long black necromancer's cloak and pictured him concocting nefarious substances in mortars and retorts, rather like that friar whom we have all seen on the stage concocting a death-brew for Romeo. But if we strip off the fancy dress and try to reach an understanding of the man as he really was, we find only a shrewd, tough, tirelessly inquisitive and irrepressibly argumentative character who lived to a ripe old age and spent a great part of it deliberately shocking people : a figure rather like that of Thomas Hobbes, though Hobbes seems to have known a little better when to stop.

He was born about 1214 and took Holy Orders before he was twenty. The cast of his mind is shown when he first of all refuses to read Aristotle in the accepted Latin translations, learns to read the original Greek and then declares that if he had his way, every translation of Aristotle would be burned.

From Aristotle in Greek he proceeds to the Arabian scientists who, in the mediaeval world, were the natural successors of the Greeks. He turns to "speculative alchemy," which he presently declares to be one of the three foundations of true science. Here already we have the foundations of the Baconian legend, although Bacon's "alchemy" was practised in as dispassionate a spirit as modern chemistry. He was known, even among his contemporaries, as the Marvellous Doctor (Doctor Admirabilis). But as he pursued his researches, it is clear that a vision dawned upon him which lifted him clean out of the surrounding world : the vision of man's future power over nature. He writes of boats which shall be driven without oars, bridges which will stand without supporting piers, self-propelled carriages and other possible mechanical inventions. At the same time, his contempt for orthodox thought, as practised in the schools of Oxford and Paris, gathers head. He takes, not only his science from the Arabians, but also his invective. He criticises a learned rival in these terms : "His works have four faults. The first is boundless, puerile vanity ; the second is ineffable falsity; the third is superfluity of bulk ... and the fourth is ignorance of the most useful and most beautiful parts of philosophy." The style, which would have delighted the taste of Haroun-Al-Rachid, fell less gratefully upon the ears of the reverend scholastics of Paris. They shut him up for ten years in 1257 ; he wrote his *Opus Majus* in prison. Scarcely had he been released when he offended again. His *Summary of Philosophical Study*, written about 1271, probably caused the second scandal. At the age of sixty-four, he was summoned before the Chapter of his Order and condemned for "making innovations" ; this time it was fourteen years' imprisonment. The aged philosopher emerged

ROGER BACON d 1294
Illumination from a fifteenth century Ms.

from prison, wrote a book upon theology and died : worthy, if any man ever was, of a philosopher's grave on British soil.

What was the system of philosophy which emerged from this stormy life ? It had two sides, negative and positive. The negative side was the rejection of contemporary methods of reasoning. Mediaeval or "scholastic" philosophy reposed, like modern law, upon precedent ; the truth had been revealed and one had only to refine upon it. Bacon dismissed this philosophy as a compound of four errors : of obsequiousness to authority, ingrained habits of thought, deference to the unlettered crowd and the empty ostentation of knowledge. The positive side of Bacon's work represents his greatest contribution to philosophy. "There are two modes in which we acquire knowledge, argument and experiment. If any man who had never seen fire were to hear proved by satisfactory argument that fire burns and destroys things, his mind would not rest satisfied, nor would he avoid fire ; until by putting his hand or some combustible thing into it, he proved by actual experiment what the argument laid down ; but after the experiment has been made, his mind receives certainty and rests in the possession of truth." A thirteeth-century philosopher who proposed to divert his learned colleagues from their transcendental hairsplitting to the practical untidy work of the laboratory, was as if a physician in the years of the Great Plague should have told his profession to cease their incantations and look for the germs.

We can better appreciate the quality of Roger Bacon by comparing him with another British Franciscan : John Duns Scotus. Duns is a Scottish village lying about halfway between Berwick and Edinburgh, almost on the English border ; here Duns Scotus is said to have been born about the year 1265. He, like Roger Bacon, studied both in Oxford and in Paris but in all probability missed the influence of the older man. He had spent four years at Paris and at least ten years in Oxford before he began the Oxford lectures on theology in 1300 which constitute one of his surviving works. Later, he lectured in Paris ; and as Bacon was termed the Marvellous Doctor, so he earned the name of the Subtle Doctor (Doctor Subtilis), a happy example of popular discernment. He was an infinitely more conventional figure, a true "scholastic," who took part in the current scholastic controversies. He argued about such matters as "the hylomorphic composition of angels." The word "dunce" (from Duns) indicates the contempt which a later age felt for the whole scholastic tradition. But even Duns Scotus disturbed men's minds in his time ; it is said that his books were publicly burned in Oxford by his philosophical opponents.

In the year of Bacon's death (1294), when Duns Scotus was at the height of his career, we read that the number of foreign students at Oxford was so great that they could not be accommodated in the city. The prestige of English scholarship was already rising fast. Two hundred years later it is no longer surprising when one of the greatest continental scholars, Erasmus, visits Cambridge. It was at Cambridge that Erasmus first met the author of *Utopia*—Sir Thomas More.

More is perhaps not strictly a philosopher. He is *anima naturaliter philosophica*. His *Utopia* which is a description of an ideal society or commonwealth, must be taken as a profound fable rather than an enquiry into the principles of knowledge. But it shows the new renaissance temper abroad in England, the switch of interest from Aristotle to Plato. And a liberal, even radical spirit of criticism. The citizens of Utopia enjoyed complete religious toleration ; they had "priests of exceeding holiness and therefore very few." They had a law that those who would marry must approve each other's naked body before the ceremony was performed. They considered war as "a thing very beastly" ; yet their women accompanied their husbands into battle. *Utopia* was published in 1516, when More was thirty-eight years old ; and with its old-fashioned Latin dress and new-fangled ideas, it stands as a bridge between Mediaevalism and the Elizabethan Age of Enterprise.

"As water ascends no higher than the level of the first spring, so knowledge derived from Aristotle will at most rise no higher than the knowledge of Aristotle." This forthright pronouncement occurs in the first philosophical work written in the English language. It demolished in one sentence the whole laboured edifice which had been raised in the Middle Ages. The author was a second Bacon, Francis, later Baron Verulam ; and the work, the *Advancement of Learning*.

The *Advancement of Learning* was published in 1605, two years after Queen Elizabeth's death. It ante-dated by 32 years the publication by Descartes of the *Discours sur la Methode*, which is conventionally regarded as the fountain-head of modern philosophy. Descartes' revolutionary method consisted in building up knowledge from the beginning by rejecting every belief which could possibly be doubted ; but Francis Bacon before him had declared : "Our one hope is to begin the whole labour of the mind again." The *Advancement of Learning* stands as a landmark, not only in British, but in European philosophical history.

Francis Bacon, even more than his namesake, presents us with a personal enigma. He, too, trails his clouds of legend. One of the wildest fables which has grown up round his name is that which credits him with the writing of Shakepeare's plays. This may at least be taken as a tribute to Bacon's vast intellectual powers. He has said many things worthy of Shakespeare. The magnificent boast : "I have taken all knowledge to be my province" might well have come from the same pen as wrote of the Roman Triumvir : "Why man he doth bestride the narrow world like a Colossus." Yet, although there is grandeur enough in Bacon, there is little lyricism and less humour. Bacon is at bottom practical. Some of his most memorable sayings are the stuff of politics. Consider this, upon war resources : "The sinews of war are not money ; if the sinews of men's arms be wanting, they are a soft and effeminate nation." Or this, upon seapower : "The being master of the sea leaves a nation at great liberty to act and to take as much or as little of the war as it pleases, whilst those who are superior in land forces have yet numerous difficulties to struggle with." How often these words are quoted without regard to the author of them !

The enigma of Francis Bacon resides in his personal character. His public career was stained continually by treachery and self-seeking. He betrayed his friend and patron, the Earl of Essex. Under King James I we see him putting neither his own integrity nor the public good before personal advancement. He schemes for the extension of the King's Prerogative and the hoodwinking of Parliament at a time when the authority of Parliament was the supreme condition for the further advancement of British liberties. Presented in a certain light, his elaborate machinations to protect the Duke of Buckingham's monopolies appear more odious than royal tyranny. He achieved his aim of becoming Lord Chancellor but was brought down by his accumulating enemies within three years. He was convicted of taking bribes in the discharge of his judicial duties. The legitimate receipts of his office were about £2,790 ; his actual income was about £16,000.

Bacon's philosophy was that of a man of the world. He says roundly of his system : "The matter in hand is no mere philosophy of speculation, but the real business and fortunes of the human race." Here, certainly, we have the note, never long absent from our island philosophy, struck with surpassing vigour and boldness. Knowledge for its own sake means nothing to Francis Bacon. Knowledge must be justified by works ; true knowledge means power over nature. It is easy to see how a man who held these views would not readily accept the status of an academic philosopher. He even says in one place, that those who spend their whole lives in writing books do so because they do not realise that there are other easier roads to fame.

It is a fantastic coincidence that Francis Bacon should have shared with a thirteenth-century predecessor not only a name but also a great part of his "new method." Francis, like Roger Bacon, discovered precisely four causes of human error. He describes Four Idols which delude the human mind : Idols of the Tribe, Idols of the Cave, Idols of the Marketplace and Idols of the Theatre. The word "idols" sounds picturesque ; it is a direct translation from Plato. The Idols of the Tribe are those fallacies which arise from the very structure of men's minds ; for example when we jump to a general conclusion on the basis of one example. The Idols of the Cave are the errors peculiar to the individual ; for example, when a man thinks a subject is specially important because he himself has studied it. The Idols of the Market are the errors caused by the misleading use of words. Nothing, as we shall see, is more up-to-date in Francis Bacon than his analysis of the fallibility of words. He says in one place : "In Physics, where nature is to be caught by works and not the adversary by argument, truth in this way slips through our fingers, because the subtlety of the operations of nature far exceeds the subtlety of words." The Idols of the Theatre are the narrow systems of philosophy which have hitherto gained currency in the world. Bacon says that time is like a river ; it brings the refuse down to us and leaves the solid stuff behind !

Then, too, Francis Bacon, like Roger, bases the new method entirely upon *experiment*. Philosophers, he says, must become like little children, examining the elements of nature. But—and this is the startling suggestion —nothing else will suffice than the assemblage of all existing instances of the object studied and no generalisation will be valid unless it is based on all the instances. Bacon realises, of course, that a literal interpretation of this method would make all generalisation impossible. He allows a sort of tentative generalisation which he calls, picturesquely, the First Vintage. In this Bacon shows remarkable anticipations of modern thought. The final generalisation, which can be made after the active researches described

FRANCIS BACON 1561-1626
Oil painting. Studio of Paul Van Somer

have been completed, Bacon calls the Form. When we have understood the form of anything, we shall be able to exploit our knowledge and achieve supremacy over nature. Such is the Baconian method or Baconian Induction as it is sometimes called.

What Bacon planned was a sequence of six mighty works; he catalogues them for us in the preface to the *Advancement of Learning*. 1. A Survey and Extension of the Sciences. This was the *Advancement of Learning,* published by Bacon, as we have seen, in 1605. 2. *Novum Organum*. This work was published in 1620. 3. *Phenomena of the Universe*. This was to be the vast natural and experimental history on which the new philosophy was to be founded. This was never written. Many writers have declared that the collection which Bacon proposed was too comprehensive to be possible. 4, 5 and 6, *Ladder of the Understanding, Precursors of the Second Philosophy* and the *Second Philosophy*, were likewise unwritten. In them Bacon imagined the development of the philosophy or science which would put all nature at man's disposal and create undreamed-of sources of power. Once again, we detect the faint spark which was to light the Industrial Revolution.

In the *Novum Organum* Bacon attempts to show the new method in operation. He applies it to the notion of heat. First he collects all the known instances of heat. It is an astonishing list, ranging from the rays of the sun, ignited meteors and volcanic flames, to "all shaggy substances," "fresh horse-dung" and even old nasturtium applied to the palate. He then collects instances where we might expect heat and find none : as from the light of the stars, from phosphorescence, and so on. Finally, he examines the variation of heat in a number of instances. As the collection of instances is acknowledged to be incomplete, he can only proceed to a tentative generalisation : the First Vintage of the Form of Heat. This Bacon defines as follows : "Heat is an expansive motion restrained, and striving to exert itself in the smaller particles." John Stuart Mill says that Bacon's mistake was in assuming that *one* cause produced all instances of heat ; in the real world there is always a multiplicity of causes.

On Easter Sunday, April 9th, 1626, Francis Bacon died, poor, dis-graced, but still experimenting. He had been riding out to Highgate, and got down from the coach to stuff a newly-killed fowl with snow ; he was investigating "the conservation and induration of bodies." He was taken ill and had to seek shelter in the house of Lord Arundel, to whom he dictated a letter of apology. "My Very Good Lord, I was likely to have had the fortune of Caius Plinius the elder, who lost his life by trying an experiment about the burning of the mountain Vesuvius." So passed Francis of Verulam, perhaps to be called first of a long line of modern European philosophers, whom Pope, in a cruel epigram, styled "the wisest, brightest, meanest of mankind."

A more generous epitaph, and one better fitted to our purpose, has been left by Charles Darwin who, more than two hundred years later, wrote that he had "worked on true Baconian principles and, without any theory, collected facts on a wholesale scale." Nothing would have more gratified the originator of the Baconian philosophy, who had wished his work to be translated into Latin for the benefit of posterity, than that his influence should have reached down the centuries and touched, among all others, the author of the *Origin of Species*.

THOMAS HOBBES 1588-1679
Engraving after Casper by Wenceslaus Hollar

III

AFTER Francis Bacon, we enter upon the Great Age of British philosophy. It was also the age which saw the mortal struggle between King and Parliament, the Puritan dictatorship of Oliver Cromwell, the Restoration and the English Revolution and the early stages of the hundred-year war with France.

The outstanding names are those of Hobbes, Locke, Berkeley and Hume. Greatness is not an easily measurable quality; and if we are to attempt to distribute it among four such competitors, we might fall into the error of Paris, who should have excused himself from passing judgment. Let us say that these four men were collectively great and ask what they collectively achieved. They broke down any intellectual basis that may have remained for controlling the free exercise of human thought. Hobbes assailed the temporal power of the Church. He was not the first nor the last to denounce ecclesiastical vested interests but he was certainly one of the most effective. Locke's work on religious and political toleration chastened the powers of civil government. He, like Milton, hated censors, the miserable creatures who imposed a tax of 6/8d. per volume upon a set of Cicero imported from Holland. From the sailing of the Mayflower in 1620 to Hume's *Dialogues upon Natural Religion* it is as if a new intellectual climate has descended upon the land. Instead of the harsh recurring frosts, there is a reign of scarcely interrupted sunshine. Such a liberation based, not on accident, but upon that fundamental effort of thought which we call philosophy, was necessary to the century of science which immediately followed and which the philosopher-pioneers foresaw.

To begin, then, with Hobbes. Hobbes as a young man used to walk with Francis Bacon in his garden. It was the pupil's task to imprison upon paper the ideas which flowed from the master's conversation ; and we hear that his lordship "better liked Mr. Hobbes taking his thoughts than any of the others because he understood what he wrote." But Hobbes was not the man to remain a taker-down of other people's thoughts for long. He was what is called in the vernacular a "character." His inordinate vanity, his eye darting like a "live bright coal," his endless disputatiousness, combined with a rare capacity for friendship, caused people to take sides for and against him even though they had never read his works. He laid down the law on all subjects indifferently. He hated bishops and all persons of unnatural unction. He was a confirmed bachelor, though he is said to have had an illegitimate daughter whom he referred to as his *delictum juventutis*. He was still publishing his latest philosophic discoveries at the age of ninety. He lived to be ninety-one. He was the George Bernard Shaw of his day.

Hobbes was by no means born into philosophy. He was lucky to get any education at all. His father was a disreputable country parson. One Sunday, after playing cards all night, he startled his congregation by waking from a snooze in the pulpit and shouting : "Spades are trumps !" Presently, after a brawl at the church door, he disappeared, deserting his family. An uncle sent the young Hobbes to Oxford, where he distinguished himself in Latin and Greek. Then, after leaving Oxford, he secured a tutorship which shaped his whole life—in the family of Lord Cavendish, later first Earl of Devonshire. He never broke his friendship with the Cavendish family ; he lived and died in their ancestral homes of Chatsworth and Hardwicke ; through them he met the Kings of Europe and, more important, the great scholars, Descartes, Galileo. He was over forty before that critical incident occurred which has, perhaps, been somewhat overdramatised. "By God !" says he, looking at a proposition of Euclid

Title Page of Hobbes' *Leviathan*, 1651

in a friend's book, "this is impossible!" But following the proof from proposition to proposition, he becomes convinced and begins to dream of establishing a philosophical system as logical and remorseless as Euclid's geometry. This philosophy took on a political bias because, says Hobbes, the country was "boiling hot with political questions, the forerunners of an approaching war." The philosophy he wanted to write would have been in three parts: the first dealing with matter, the second with human nature and the third with society. Actually he carried out something like this plan; only in the stress of the Civil War, he wrote the last part first. This was *Leviathan*: Hobbes' masterpiece and one of the great monuments of the English language. The first part of the system, the analysis of matter, was developed in a later book *De Corpore*, written in Latin; and much of what Hobbes had to say about human nature was telescoped into *Leviathan* and an earlier work upon the social organisation of man *De Cive*. Hobbes was, in the strict philosophical sense, a materialist. He believed that nothing existed except matter—matter in motion. Just as he ascribed the phenomena of Nature to the ceaseless motion of its elements, so he thought he could reduce all human affairs to "the internal motions of men"; he was an exponent of that oldest Greek philosophy which dismissed all reality in the words πάντα ῥεῖ—everything flows. Something in the primeval iconoclasm of this doctrine appealed to Hobbes' temperament.

Hobbes wrote to hurt and counted nothing well said which did not strike a telling blow against someone or something. Consider some of his typical pronouncements. That the first passion which inclines men to peace is fear of death. That the essence of commonwealth is rule by terror. That the only difference between monarchy and tyranny or between democracy and anarchy resides in the outlook of the governed. That liberty consists in submission to the monarch. That the prosperity of a people depends, not on their form of government, but on their obedience, and that those who preach disobedience and revolution as a means to reform are like the daughters of Peleus who, desiring to renew the youth of their decrepit father, cut him in pieces and boiled him but made not of him a new man. That a man may deny the true God at the command of his sovereign, because profession with the tongue is but an external thing. That a king must either rule or be ruled by the Pope because the distinction of temporal and spiritual power is but words. And so on.

These are some of the findings of *Leviathan*, in which the essence of Hobbes' thought is concentrated. Leviathan is the name given by Hobbes to the "mortal power" exercised by governments. The political theory of the book can be summarised quite simply: it is that the natural man, swayed only by selfish passions, must be for ever at war with his fellows unless he *contracts* to submit to Leviathan, that is, to a *sovereign*, conceived as an absolute and external power. The contract is cemented by *fear*. The reduction of all human activities to selfish elements is so ruthlessly urged and argued, with such savage excursions against certain social groups, like the clergy and the universities, that parts of *Leviathan* read like a forerunner of Freud's analytical psychology, and parts like a Shaw preface. The book was published in 1651 to greet the first years of Cromwell's dictatorship. It was not unacceptable to the rulers of the Restoration. But of the opinion of the mass of the people we can perhaps best judge by the fact that, after the Great Plague of 1665 when God's displeasure became a matter of public enquiry and concern, *Leviathan* narrowly escaped suppression by Act of Parliament.

Hobbes' unorthodoxy flashed like a meteor through the sky dazzling the beholder ; Locke put a new star among the constellations which has never ceased to light men's way. Locke was nineteen years old when *Leviathan* was published. His *Two Treatises of Government* were directed, not against Hobbes, but against a lesser disciple of Hobbes, Sir Robert Filmer ; yet ever and again, by a turn of phrase or a pointed allusion, Locke shows himself conscious of the older master-spirit. I take the innermost essence of Locke's political philosophy to be contained in this proposition : "He who attempts to get another man into his absolute power does thereby put himself into a state of war with him." This superb declaration may be found in the seventeenth paragraph of the second *Treatise*. From this follows Locke's view of monarchy, that wherever the King may be found exercising absolute power over his subjects, whether he be called the Czar or the Grand Signior, such a society is the most primitive possible. From this follows the memorable dictum which justifies war and in extreme cases revolution : "May the commands, then, of a prince be opposed ? To this I answer, that force is to be opposed to nothing but to unjust and to unlawful force." Locke held the very moderate view that government was a responsibility delegated by the community for the purpose of protecting each member's life and property. Its function was to safeguard, not to restrict, the liberty of the individual. The *Epistle on Toleration* (*Epistola de Tolerantia*, one of the last English philosophical works to be published in Latin) carried the same theme ; and if, as is sometimes pointed out, he himself failed to tolerate Papists and Atheists, he surely hastened the day of their toleration.

Locke, too, had a sounder initiation into government than Hobbes, the tutor of earls and princes. He was born in a cottage. He was by turns doctor, university professor, diplomat, civil servant ; and he was turned out of a university post by one of the arbitrary acts of King James II. When the revolution broke out, Locke had been seven years in exile in Holland. He returned in the same ship which carried the Princess Mary and was invited to become William of Orange's Ambassador to one of the German capitals, Berlin and Vienna. Nothing is more revealing of Locke's personal character than the letter in which he declined this employment.

What is most serious in the letter is too long to be quoted ; but like Ambassador Dodd of the United States, apprehensive of the summons to adapt himself to the habits of the Nazi leaders, Locke takes alarm at the German reputation for hard drinking. "It is no small matter in such stations to be acceptable to the people one has to do with, in being able to accommodate oneself to their fashions. I should think it more for the King's interest to send a man of equal parts that could drink his share than the soberest man in the kingdom."

Modest, efficient, scholarly, democratic (his father fought in the Civil War on the Parliament side)—these qualities would have inevitably ranged him against Hobbes, would have gone far to account for his essays on political matters and the kindred work *Some Thoughts Concerning Education* in which he makes many practical and modern-sounding suggestions for forming the minds of children. They would never explain that towering intellectual achievement, the first full study of the nature and limits of philosophic knowledge in modern times, the *Essay on Human Understanding*. Locke came to this by a sort of revelation. The scene was such a one as Plato often describes and Locke's description of it is strikingly similar. Five or six of his friends were talking in his room about morality and religion. "It came into my thoughts that we took a wrong course, and that before we set ourselves upon enquiries of that nature, it was necessary to examine our abilities and see what objects our understandings were, or were not, fitted to deal with." Locke parted from his friends that night with the promise that he would write down his thoughts upon these first principles. The task took him nearly twenty years.

What Locke did was to map the human mind. Like the old geographers who charted Africa, he coasted patiently from bay to bay, measuring distances, dropping his plummet into every firth and inlet and, on occasion, making exploratory forays into the interior. The immense and original labour which Locke performed opened up a new philosophical continent. None of his successors but was constrained at some time or another to say : "John Locke travelled this way before me"; they acknowledged his achievement by the glee with which they corrected a detail here and there in his plan.* Locke made certain large assumptions. He called all the objects of the human understanding *ideas* and treated them neutrally. That is to say, *seeing a tree* and *thinking about God* were both *ideas*, according to Locke ; and it was wildly exhilarating in the seventeenth century that anyone should hold the balance so evenly before dropping two such traditionally uneven ideas upon the scales. Next, he regarded the mind as a blank upon which the ideas were imposed, like pictures on a screen. There were no such things as innate ideas ; all ideas entered the mind from outside, although some of them, the compound and abstract ones, had been worked up by the mind, as raw material is worked up into a

*Locke's map is not inaccurately drawn even by to-day standards.

JOHN LOCKE

Oil painting by Sir Godfrey Kneller, 1646 - 1723

EDINBURGH FROM THE WEST, IN THE TIME OF DAVID HUME

Coloured engraving by Paul Sandby, 1725 - 1809

complex finished product. Perhaps his most characteristic assumption was that the ideas sit somewhere midway between the mind and the external world. This is the very battleground of philosophy, the question what is the relation between the mind and its ideas and between ideas and external things. Locke said that the ideas were "in the mind" and that some ideas "resembled" external things ; that was as far as he went into the matter. But one cannot in the same voyage circumnavigate a continent and trace all its rivers to the source.

He takes his ideas, then, and examines them from various angles, holds them up to the light, so to speak. First, he classifies them according to their origins. Ideas originate from *sensation* or *reflection* or both. The ideas of sensation are, of course, the shapes, colours, tastes and smells which come to us from the outside world. For example, we look at the sun. We have various ideas of roundness, whiteness, and heat : all simple ideas of sensation. The roundness is a *primary quality*, *resembling* something in the sun ; because although it may not be the real size and shape of the sun, yet the sun has *some* size and shape. The whiteness and heat are *secondary qualities*, because these are wholly begotten upon the mind by the senses and neither they nor anything like them exist in the sun. The distinction which Locke made between primary and secondary qualities stirred up a philosophic controversy which has lasted to this day. The ideas of reflection appear when our mental faculties of memory, will-power, discernment, knowledge and so on begin to work upon the raw material of sensation. When we remember the sun and when we deliberately think of the sun, we have simple ideas of reflection. When we bask in the sun, we have an idea of pleasure ; when we are blistered by the sun, we have an idea of pain : and these are also simple ideas, but of sensation and reflection mixed.

We come next to the complex ideas. The sun is, of course, itself a complex idea ; it is an idea of something which is at once round and white and hot. The mind constantly builds collections of qualities like these into ideas of *substance*, from which is finally built our idea of the world of nature. It compares one idea with another to produce ideas of *relations* ; for example, we say "Queen Elizabeth lived 69 years," an idea which we get by comparing the duration of one substance (Queen Elizabeth) with 69 annual revolutions of another substance (the sun). The mind also has the power of abstraction, that is to say, it can combine ideas regardless of their relations with things. The ancients produced their idea of a Sun God by combining the ideas of the sun and of a very powerful man. Locke rightly saw that language itself is an act of abstraction and that to call every leaf on every tree in the world by a particular name would be the very negation of language, because no man would understand what another was saying. There is a very modern spirit in the way Locke bases much of his reasoning on the behaviour of animals and young children. He reminds us in one passage how children invent their own words to represent their real ideas of things, reversing the habit of parsons and schoolmasters who repeat other men's gibberish with the utmost persuasiveness in spite of the fact that it represents nothing really existing in nature.

After assembling the contents of the mind (and no brief summary could so much as suggest the vigour and richness of the detail), Locke asks: "What is knowledge and how much can we be said to know?" To the first question: "What is knowledge?" he answers that knowledge consists in the agreement which we perceive between our ideas, or the agreement which we perceive between our ideas and reality. We know that two plus two equals four because this idea agrees with all other ideas and never comes up against an idea that two plus two equals five or fifty. We know that the sun exists because our idea of the sun agrees with something real in the outside world. Locke held that knowledge of substances, that is to say, the outside world, was very incomplete. We knew substances only through sensation; and to find out that the sun hardened mud but melted wax required patient observation and experiment. Beyond the region of our certain knowledge, said Locke, stretched a twilight region in which the judgment operated. We could judge of many things which we did not know, but only on probability. Of the pitfalls which beset the fallible judgment of man, Locke tells a story which he must have heard with delight during his residence in Holland. The Dutch Ambassador to the Court of Siam was trying to explain to the Siamese King how the northern rivers froze in winter time; the ice was so thick, he said, that an elephant could stand on it. But the King of Siam, applying his own system of probabilities, was merely confirmed in his previous belief that the Dutch Ambassador was a liar.

Locke put the problem of knowledge upon a psychological basis. Indeed the *Essay* may be read as the first great study in analytical psychology. It has, as we have already indicated, a truly superb completeness. It is not hard to lose one's way in the *Essay*; but it is extremely hard to find any point which Locke has entirely neglected. Many of the criticisms of Locke fail before the simple fact that Locke himself answered them, but in a different place. This applies not only to the criticisms of the egregious Bishop of Worcester, to whom Locke made three public rejoinders, but even to Berkeley and Hume who owed to Locke the main body of their theses. The *Essay* must, in fact, be one of the world's hardest books to index properly. Locke is not over logical. He will never force a fact to fit his theory. Locke's habit of walking round his subject and commenting on it from various directions makes for occasional inconsistencies, which are the professional critic's delight. The whole is dominated by the intense conviction that philosophy is for use, not for empty debate. If knowledge be a sun, let us work in sunlight; if a candle, by candlelight: but let us work!

GEORGE BERKELEY 1685-1753
Oil painting by Vanderbank

The Bishop of Worcester's fears were not unjustified. The young took up the New Philosophy with enthusiasm, even the future bishops. A twenty-year old theological student of Trinity College, Dublin, organised a study-circle to discuss the *Essay on Human Understanding*. It was George Berkeley, later Bishop of Cloyne. This engaging young Irishman—for that he was engaging we have more tangible evidence than his charm of style—believed that he could resolve the difficulties and uncertainties of the famous *Essay* by a single stroke of intuition. In 1710, when he was only twenty-five, he published the *Principles of Human Knowledge*. His three best-known philosophical works, the *Theory of Vision*, the *Principles* and the *Dialogues Between Hylas and Philonous* were all written before he was thirty. After that, his interests in philosophy slackened as his ecclesiastical career matured. His later books, which mix Christian apologetics and Platonic mysticism, are of interest only to the specialist.

What was the young man's inspiration which was to make all Locke plain sailing ? Berkeley assailed the New Philosophy at its weakest point, the junction between the *idea*, which Locke said was in the mind, and the *thing* which the idea represented and which was assumed to exist in a world outside the mind. Why, asked Berkeley, if all that the mind knows is its own ideas, do we assume that an outside world exists at all ? "Some truths there are so near and obvious to the mind that a man need only open his eyes to see them. Such I take this important one to be, that all the choir of heaven and furniture of the earth, in a word, all those bodies which compose the mighty frame of the world, have not any subsistence without a mind, that their *being* is *to be perceived*, that, consequently, so long as they are not actually perceived by me or do not exist in my mind or that of any other created spirit, they must either have no existence at all or else subsist in the mind of some external spirit."

Two amusing comments on Berkeley's theory may be recalled. One of them is the immortal anecdote about Doctor Johnson. "After we came out of church," says Boswell, "we stood for some time talking of Bishop Berkeley's ingenious sophistry to prove the non-existence of matter, and that everything in the universe is merely ideal. I observed that, though we are satisfied his doctrine is not true, it is impossible to refute it. I shall never forget the alacrity with which Johnson answered, striking his foot with mighty force against a large stone, till he rebounded from it : "I refute it thus !' " It may be pointed out in Johnson's defence that Bertrand Russell borrows the essential part of his argument when, after observing that Berkeley is "very hard to refute," he adds that his commonsense revolts against the consequences.

Less reasonable but more witty is the limerick attributed to an Oxford professor :

"There was a young man who said 'God
Must find it exceedingly odd
    That this sycamore tree
    Just ceases to be
When there's no-one about in the Quad'."

This limerick, like the equally celebrated one about Einstein's Theory of Relativity, is unfair. Berkeley never maintained that the sycamore tree simply ceased to exist when there was no-one looking at it. What he said was that the "matter" or "substance" or whatever was supposed to cause the greenness of the leaves and the jagged shape of the branches and to persist when there was no image of a sycamore in any mind *did not exist at all or at any time*. But the whole sensible world of Nature did exist, not only during the transient perceptions of men, but also permanently, in the ideas of God. Nature was a manifestation of God's ideas; and there are passages in Berkeley which approximate to the extreme Spinozan view, that Nature *is* God.

Berkeley is important in the history of philosophy because he produced a very pure form of a theory which constantly recurs in philosophic literature under the general title of *Idealism*. This theory represents the Universe as of mental stuff and is opposed to *Materialism*, which represents the Universe as basically material and derives all mental phenomena from the motions and properties of matter. Hobbes was an out-and-out Materialist; Berkeley an equally thoroughgoing Idealist. The key work is the *Principles* from which we have already quoted the key-passage. Second ranks *Hylas and Philonous*, in which the three main ingredients of his life-work are all attractively deployed : the Idealist theory, which was his own ; the arguments, which were broadly Locke's ; and the manner which was Plato's.

> *Philonous :* Can any doctrine be true that necessarily leads a man into an absurdity ?
> *Hylas :* Without doubt it cannot.
> *Philonous :* Is it not an absurdity to think that the same thing should be at the same time both cold and warm ?
> *Hylas :* It is.
> *Philonous :* Suppose now one of your hands hot and the other cold, and that they are both at once put into the same vessel of tepid water, will not the water seem cold to one hand and warm to the other ?
> *Hylas :* It will.
> *Philonous :* Ought we not therefore by your principles to conclude it is really both cold and warm at the same time, that is, according to your own concession, to believe an absurdity ?

Berkeley makes a brilliant splash upon the pages of British philosophy but with a talent which shines, perhaps, a little too smooth and easy against Locke's rugged genius.

Hume rounded off the Great Age. The *Treatise of Human Nature*, which was to jerk all European philosophy into a new groove, ripened as young as Berkeley's masterpiece. It was begun in 1734 when Hume was twenty-three and finished three years later. If he had not written it then, the world would almost certainly have lost it altogether, for Hume craved for popular fame and when he discovered that philosophy did not bring it, he turned to other subjects. In later years he was so ashamed of the neglect into which the *Treatise* had fallen that he set himself to rewrite it in a more popular style. Such are the aberrations to which even the most powerful mind is liable.

Hume was of a simple, generous, gentle nature—sharper in his writings than in his dealings with mankind. His friend Adam Smith, the author of *The Wealth of Nations*, declared after Hume's death that he was an example of the wise and good man. Yet there was a ruling vanity in Hume which, if less assertive and angular than that of Hobbes, at least suffices to make his virtues interesting. It may be seen in the brief autobiographical sketch he left behind him, *My Own Life;* and his letters from Paris, describing the compliments which the Dauphin and Madame de Pompadour showered upon him, are models of eighteenth-century complacency. Poor Hume, who wrote to Hippolyte, Comtesse de Boufflers : "Commonsense requires that I should keep at a distance from all attachments that can imply passion !" Not Gibbon himself spurned a lover with more self-consciousness or less charm.

My Own Life is what we should call nowadays a literary success-story. Hume spent his mature powers upon three massive English Histories and fitted in, so to speak, his occasional digressions into Philosophy and Religion. Twice he held public appointments. From 1746 to 1748 he was aide-de-camp to General St. Clair. He took part in a "Commando" raid against L'Orient on the coast of Brittany. He also accompanied a British Military Mission to the Courts of Vienna and Turin ; he has left in his letters a fascinating account of the Court of Maria Theresa, the goitre in the Bavarian valleys, the lovely Slovene countryside and his homage at Virgil's birthplace. Then from 1763 to 1765 he was Secretary to the Embassy in Paris, for a few months actually Chargé d'Affaires. He presents these two episodes of public service as interruptions in a scholar's life ; and he comments here and there upon royalties and copyright payments in the modern manner. He is very conscious of his "public." At first they reject him ; generally they are violently agitated by him ; but all goes right in the end. The *Treatise of Human Nature* "fell dead-born from the press" ; but in the final years "the copy-money given me by the booksellers much exceeded anything formerly known in England."

The great *Treatise* has the marks of youth upon it. It begins weakly. There is a sort of insolence in places—much talk of "profound reasoning," a gulf like a caste-system fixed between "philosophic" and "vulgar" minds, no acknowledgment of the debt to Locke, of which the most casual reader must be instantly conscious. For Hume takes over entire that part of Locke's system which atomises the mind into *ideas*, except that he calls Locke's ideas of sensation *impressions*. He even attempts a superficial catalogue of his *ideas* and *impressions* in the Lockian manner. But these are preliminary hesitations : we are soon to launch once more into uncharted seas. We are going to apply Locke's psychological method with a subtlety and accuracy for which Locke had no time and from the consequences of which he would have certainly shrunk. *Ideas*, such as the abstract one of "humanity," differ from *impressions*, such as "seeing the sun," only because the idea is faint and the impression vivid and strong. The fact that I believe that the sun exists, while I do not believe that "humanity" in the abstract exists, is, for Hume, simply a sign of the

DAVID HUME 1711-1776
Oil painting by Allan Ramsay

vividness of the impression as against the idea—certainly not a proof of
the existence of a physical sun. If any impression or idea strikes in on
our minds with particular force, we are said to believe it ; this, according
to Hume, is all that knowledge means. And further : we believe what we
believe out of habit. For example, when we believe that the sun will rise
to-morrow, our belief is simply a strong idea, based upon the habit of
observing the sun rise upon innumerable morrows in the past. Thus, for
all natural laws, based on the operation of cause and effect, Hume substitutes
simply a *feeling* of belief, based on habit. It was this destructive criticism
of the idea of cause which set Kant's mind working. For if one could not
be, but only *feel*, certain that the sun would rise next day, it would seem
that all science was illusory and indeed impossible.

31

We have no space here to follow the *Treatise* along all its ramifications. But to take a specimen of Hume's method : his treatment of the problem of the external world. Locke had, as we have seen, assumed that there was an external world, corresponding in some respects to our ideas of it. Berkeley had declared that there was no need to assume an external world at all—at least, not in the usual sense of the term. Hume said : since philosophers agree that all we can know is our own ideas and since we are not in direct contact with the external world at any point, how do we come by this extraordinary notion ? Note the form of the question—not how can the notion be justified, but how do we come by it. Well, the philosopher looks at his desk and papers ; here they are, here they were yesterday and the day before. He looks at the fire ; it certainly has sunk since he last looked at it, but by natural degrees, so that it is visibly "the same fire." From these observations, Hume concludes that when certain impressions return to us, either unchanged (like the desk) or with expected and coherent changes (like the fire), our imagination (like a boat which continues in movement when the oars are lifted) insists on filling in the spaces between the interrupted impressions and making one identical object out of them. Hume then refines upon this analysis. Where do we get this idea of "one identical object ?" The only identical object of which we have experience is an uninterrupted perception. (Hume now uses Berkeley's word "perception" instead of his own "impression"). If, now, we have a succession of interrupted but similar perceptions (as when we "see the sun" on several occasions) and if imagination fills in the gaps between them, we still only have one identical *perception*, not an external object. But a human mind, according to Hume, is simply a bundle or chain of perceptions (how close we are to modern forms of mental theory at this point) ; so there is no difficulty in supposing that perceptions may go on existing outside the mind. This, in fact, is exactly what the imagination does suppose when it jumps the gap between similar perceptions ; and "external object" is simply the *name* we give to these imaginatively externalised perceptions. Finally, we *believe* in external objects because the *strong feeling* which accompanies our perceptions is communicated to the figment which fills the gaps, as the lover who kisses his mistress's handkerchief feels the same passion as when he kisses her lips. The upshot of the argument is to destroy our belief in external objects altogether.

The second part of the *Treatise* deals more specifically with human nature and society. It begins, characteristically, with an analysis of the emotions of *pride* and *humility*. Hume, like Hobbes, considers that the motives which activate human behaviour are essentially selfish ; but unlike Hobbes, he finds room for an emotion of *benevolence* or *sympathy*. This part of the *Treatise*, somewhat neglected nowadays, is very important in philosophical history for its influence upon Jeremy Bentham and J. S. Mill. Similarly, the *Dialogues on Natural Religion* are important as the fore-

By courtesy of the Parker Gallery, London

LINCOLN'S INN, OF WHICH BENTHAM BECAME A MEMBER IN 1817
Coloured engraving by J. Marsh

THE LIBRARY OF TRINITY COLLEGE, DUBLIN
Berkeley was Fellow and Scholar of Trinity
Coloured engraving published by Robert Sayer, c.1760

runners of Victorian free thought and agnosticism. In these *Dialogues*, Hume chiefly assails that celebrated "argument from design" which attempts to prove the existence of God by the evidence of divine handiwork in the world of nature. He comes to the apparently cynical conclusion that the difference of opinion between the theist and the atheist is only a *verbal* one. It is a dispute, not about facts, but about degrees, as one might dispute whether Cleopatra was a beautiful or a very beautiful woman. The theist and the atheist have no deeper quarrel about the Universe, for if the one calls it incomprehensively divine, the other must acknowledge it divinely incomprehensible.

Yet Hume's very negativeness and scepticism have an underlying fire and passion. I still remember how, as a young man, I lay one evening on the river-bank at Cambridge, reading the last pages of the metaphysical section of the *Treatise*, while the summer sun climbed down ; and how I stared over the golden fields, inundated with despair that all was illusion, that nothing could be surely known. And at the same time I felt a surge of exultation that any man should have plumbed the very abyss of doubt and that I should have followed him there. No modern thinker touches like Hume that nerve of the spirit which caused Alcibiades to say of philosophy that it stings like a viper when it gets hold of a young and not insensitive mind.

> "The *intense* view of these manifold contradictions and imperfections in human reason has so wrought upon me, and heated my brain, that I am ready to reject all belief and reasoning, and can look upon no opinion even as more probable or likely than another. Where am I, or what ? From what causes do I derive my existence, and to what condition shall I return ? Whose favour shall I court, and whose anger must I dread ? What beings surround me ? and on whom have I any influence, or who have any influence on me ? I am confounded with all these questions, and begin to fancy myself in the most deplorable condition imaginable, environed with the deepest darkness, and utterly deprived of the use of every member and faculty."

Hume is a protagonist of the eighteenth-century cult of Reason. Gibbon, the arch-sceptic, had still to reach his prime—Gibbon who said that a letter of praise from Hume overpaid him for ten years of work. But this quotation from the First Book of the *Treatise* belongs rather to the succeeding age. It has more than a little in common with the poet who wrote :

> " 'Tis we, who, lost in stormy visions, keep
> With phantoms an unprofitable strife,
> And in mad trance strike with our spirit's knife
> Invulnerable nothings."

It belongs to the age when even philosophy was required to become romantic.

ADAM SMITH 1723-1790
Engraving by Kay from the *Wealth of Nations*.   Edition of 1853

IV

AFTER Hume, the Muse of Philosophy transferred her main residence across the Rhine.   Naked and unashamed she would go no
longer ; she developed a taste for showy dress.

Kant, Fichte, Hegel, Schopenhauer and Nietzsche—these were the
prophets of the new order.   In modern times, when the pendulum has

34

swung back again, it is not easy to do them justice. All dabbled in the prophetic extravagance ; and some went in up to their necks. They did not proceed by simple observation ; they thought they could dredge up truth by devising new logical implements. Kant, for example, argued like this : space must be infinite ; space cannot be infinite ; therefore space does not exist in the real world. He arrived at a real world peopled only by *Noumena*, beings more unreal than any imagined by any other philosopher. Did these German philosophers make any permanent contribution to their science to match their immense contemporary prestige ? Kant was the greatest of them ; yet what, in essence, is the *Critique of Pure Reason* but a restatement of Berkeley's Idealism in more laboured terms, with the *Noumena* replacing God ? According to Bertrand Russell, Kant was a philosophic disaster !

In Britain we have, first, a period of applied philosophy. The metaphysical enquiries of the Great Age had cleared men's minds, even if they had not entirely satisfied them ; and Adam Smith, Jeremy Bentham, John Stuart Mill and Herbert Spencer, like generals who have got a secure base of operations, all crossed that indeterminate frontier which divides pure philosophy from the social sciences. Then came the full impact of the German philosophy. Carlyle was one of its chief missionaries in England. A generation of British philosophers wrote volumes entitled *A Text-Book to Kant, The Secret of Hegel*, and so on. T. H. Green's *Prolegomena* (1883) and F. H. Bradley's *Appearance and Reality* (1893) marked the climax and close of this period.

Adam Smith (1723-1790) was, like Hume, a Scot. He became Professor of Moral Philosophy at Glasgow, resigned this post after twelve years in order to travel, and in 1776, the year of Hume's death, published *The Wealth of Nations*. No philosophic work so simple in form, so immense in scope, had been written in English since Locke's *Essay*. It was the world's first full-length study of the foundations of an industrial society. Leeds, Halifax, Sheffield, Birmingham and Wolverhampton already shadow forth their giant mechanised future ; and France, Spain, the New World, India and China all supply the author with examples and arguments. Smith believed in free trade. He believed that every man's desire to better his condition would ensure continuous economic progress, if all artificial obstructions were removed. In this book of 1776 you will find a concrete plan for universal elementary education, based on the existing Scottish system of parish schools. What is said on the subject of philosophy is interesting. Smith thought that philosophy took a wrong turn when, under the influence of ecclesiastical vested interests, the ancient division into natural philosophy (science), moral philosophy (ethics) and logic was abandoned in favour of metaphysics. For the ancient division conformed to the nature of things, but metaphysics was a "cobweb science" of churchmen's disputations.

35

London bred Jeremy Bentham (1748-1832), as well as several generations of Benthams before him. His father was a prominent member of the Scriveners' Company, well-to-do ; and Jeremy was that alarming thing, an infant prodigy. At the advanced age of three he was to be observed poring over Rapin's *History of England* ; at five he wrote Latin and had already been nicknamed "Philosopher" ; at eight he spoke French and resorted to Voltaire for light reading. As might be expected, he was a delicate, retiring child. The only out-of-the-way incident of his life was a two-year visit to Russia where one of his brothers was employed as an engineer. A friend wrote of him : "He never knew prosperity or adversity, passion or satiety. He never had even the experience which sickness gives. He lived from childhood to the age of eighty-two in boyish health. He knew no dejection, no heaviness of heart. He was a boy to the last."

Out of this temperamental serenity sprang the *greatest happiness* principle, the foundation-stone of the Utilitarian philosophy. Of course, Bentham was not the first to identify good with happiness ; there have been systems of hedonism since the world began. The opening sentence of his *Principles of Morals and Legislation* : "Nature has placed mankind under the governance of two sovereign masters, pain and pleasure" derives directly from Part Two of Hume's *Treatise*. But Bentham was a great populariser. He not only enunciated his principle ; he worked it out. He gathered disciples.

Bentham reckoned that if the *greatest happiness* principle were to be an effective guide to human action, we ought to be able to measure happiness, as we measure a table or a wall. He therefore set out seven dimensions of pleasure as follows :

1. Intensity.
2. Duration.
3. Certainty.
4. Propinquity.
5. Fecundity (or the chance it has of being followed by other pleasures).
6. Purity (or the chance it has of *not* being followed by pains).
7. Extent (that is, the number of people affected by it).

Bentham allowed for differences in human constitution ; there would be different pleasures for different people ; but all would be measured by the same standards. Let us take a simple pleasure like "smelling a wall-flower." For Bentham this pleasure was very intense, because it reminded him of his grandmother's garden at Barking. It would not rank high for duration ; but certainty and propinquity would be 100% while the smelling went on. It would be fecund if it put Bentham into a good temper for the rest of the day. It would be pure enough ; but its extent would be limited, especially if it induced a mood of solitary contemplation instead of active good works. On the other hand, the pleasure of "hating your landlady," if it was a pleasure, would probably be a faint one ; its duration

JEREMY BENTHAM 1748-1832
Drawing by G. F. Watts

might be long, but it would be very impure, especially if, as a result of
it, she brought you your shaving-water cold every morning. Add up all
the pleasures and pains consequent upon any act, and according to whether
the balance is pleasurable or painful, the act is good or bad. Two para-
doxes now confronted the author of this system. Obviously, if good *meant*
having pleasurable effect, there could not be such a thing as a bad motive.
Motives like "lust" and "avarice" were, according to Bentham, simply

37

neutral motives, "sexual desire" and "pecuniary interest," which were after-wards found to have had unpleasant effects. The second paradox was that if good was to be measured by *quantity* of pleasure, you could not say that any pleasure was *better* than another but only *greater*. Hence Bentham's notorious dictum : "Pushpin is as good as poetry." Pushpin was a child's game on the moral level of tiddlywinks. The later Utilitarians rejected this extreme consequence of Bentham's theory and admitted a *qualitative* difference between pleasures.

Bentham early resolved that his philosophy should itself conform to Utilitarian theory and be judged by its results. He wrote very little for publication ; his *Fragment on Government* and his *Introduction to the Principles of Morals and Legislation* are the books by which he is most often remembered ; but he never ceased compiling notes for his voluminous schemes of legislative reform. He had the ambition of legislating for the world ; not only the Russians and Americans, but also the Spaniards, Greeks, French, Portuguese, Mexicans and others received an offer of services ; the French gave him their citizenship and the British £23,000 in recognition of his zeal. At one time he aspired to a seat in Parliament. As he grew older, he became a political oracle, consulted especially by the men of radical views. His influence was felt in the Reform Bill, which passed into law only a few days after his death in 1832. He set political liberty high on his list of pleasures, and he considered that the only good Government in the world was that of the United States (of the rest he said that the British was the least bad). When Alexander Wedderburn, Attorney General and later Lord Chancellor of England, expressed the view that Bentham's political opinions were dangerous, Bentham retorted : "In a Government which had for its end the greatest happiness of the greatest number, Alexander Wedderburn might have been Attorney General and then Chancellor ; but he would not have been Attorney General with £15,000 a year, nor Chancellor with £25,000 and with 500 sinecures at his disposal."

John Stuart Mill stood to Bentham as Plato to Socrates. His father, James Mill, had been one of the earliest converts to the *greatest happiness* principle, and Bentham's best friend ; and John Stuart was brought up in the atmosphere of the Bentham household. He was educated by his father. A full account of this most extraordinary of all educations has been left us in Mill's *Autobiography*. His whole childhood consisted in reading classical books and taking improving walks with his father. For precocity, he out-Benthamed Bentham. He learned Greek at three. At seven he read the *Euthyphron* and five other dialogues of Plato. At eight he was teaching his sister Latin. During the walks, his father used to show him how to distinguish good arguments from bad and how to conceal his lack of religious conviction from other people. The marvel is that enough freshness was left in the child's mind to react to Bentham's Utili-

JOHN STUART MILL 1806-1873
Oil painting by G. F. Watts, 1874

tarian philosophy at fifteen years old with a sense of shock. The *greatest happiness* principle struck Mill as the final word in the science of ethics.

The rigid exclusion of all that the run of mankind calls pleasure left a certain dust of dryness upon Mill's work. His intellectual pride, his very exactness of style always limited his humanity a little ; and it was not until he married, late in life, that his broadest sympathies were released. To this period belong all Mill's labours for the oppressed. He was elected to Parliament, after warning his constituents that he would do nothing for their special interests but only what he considered to be right. He

39

was an advocate of women's suffrage and secured eighty votes in its favour from a hostile House of Commons ; the essay *On the Subjection of Women* followed three years afterwards. He fought a two years' battle for the rights of the negroes and mulattoes of Jamaica. Finally, Mill became a champion of the working people of Britain. He was the first who ever waived royalties on his books so that they should be published cheaply enough for the poor to buy. The picture survives of this most bookish of philosophers, preserved as a boy from contacts even with children of his own age, addressing a working-class audience and being asked by a heckler whether in one of his pamphlets he had not written that working men were liars. "Yes," said Mill "I wrote it." The whole audience cheered him. But he was not returned a second time to Parliament. "What was surprising," says Mill justly, "is that I should have been elected once."

The stuff of Mill's philosophy is contained in the *System of Logic*, published in 1843 when Mill was 37 years old. Now the small boy who trotted obediently at his father's heels, learning the frailties of human reason, is of an age to lay down the laws of thought for other people. His starting-point is the "proposition"—that is to say, the form of words in which we make any statement. He holds that all propositions are reducible to five primary types and that all, even the most abstract, like "Prudence is a virtue," refer to something particular in the real world. He next analyses the inductive process by which we pass from one proposition to another in enlarging our knowledge—how, for example, can we justify our "universal" scientific laws ? Mill is as suspicious as Locke and Hume before him of anything which claims to be "universal" : scientific laws must be considered approximations, based upon collections of particular instances—though Mill does not go so far as to deny the operation of invariable causes in the material world. What is the material world ? Mill affects to decline the ultimate metaphysical problems. He looks at his table (most British philosophers who address themselves to the mystery of matter begin by staring at the table !) and is content to define matter as the unknown cause of our sensations. Logic, he says, has no business with metaphysics ; on this excuse he often breaks off an argument at its most interesting point. The *System of Logic* ends with a discussion of fallacies and a long review of previous theories of knowledge ; it is, perhaps, the first book which puts into perspective what we now call modern European philosophy.

Herbert Spencer, the Philosopher of Evolution, is more difficult to classify. He believed in what H. G. Wells would call a World Brain. He published in March 1860 the prospectus of a gigantic Encyclopaedia in five parts : *First Principles ; Principles of Biology ; Principles of Psychology; Principles of Sociology* and *Principles of Morality*. The obvious comparison is with Francis Bacon's six-fold Ladder of Philosophy, with the

J. H. BRADLEY
Oil painting by W. H. Eves

J. M. E. M'TAGGART

Oil painting by Roger Fry, 1866-1934

important difference that what Herbert Spencer promised he performed. There is no consistent metaphysical point of view in Spencer's chain of treatises ; but there is a striking dominant idea. He had definitely conceived a theory of evolution before Darwin's *Origin of Species* appeared. He believed that there was a fundamental process at work in Nature : a sort of gathering together and blossoming of material particles. As in the Universe vast nebulae shrank into suns and planets, and planets shrank until they burst into life, so separate living things should be conceived as substances which were forever concentrating and liberating new energies. Spencer believed that everything in the world, even human behaviour, was developing upon this principle. Year by year he carried the mighty labour forward, publishing *First Principles* in 1862, when he was forty-two years old, and concluding with the *Principles of Ethics*, the second volume of which appeared in 1892, when he was seventy-two. No-one in modern times has read Herbert Spencer all through. (Doubtless someone will write to *The Times* contradicting this statement). He raised a monument of mental industry which recalls the pyramids of Egypt. There they stand ; but no-one will be tempted to build in the same way again.

Traces of the contemporary German vogue may be found all over Spencer's books. Such phrases as "All our knowledge is of the phenomenal" are pure Kant. It is time to look briefly at those British philosophers who swam with the full current of the alien tradition. Sir William Hamilton, to whom Mill devoted his *Examination of Sir William Hamilton's Philosophy*, was the first of them ; but T. H. Green was probably the most important. Green had worked at Heidelberg University but spent most of his life at Oxford, finally becoming Professor of Moral Philosophy there. His earliest works were destructive criticisms of Locke and Hume. "Shut up your Mill and Spencer" he told his pupils, "and open your Kant and Hegel." There was a moral force in the man which gained him universal respect and enthusiastic disciples. But although his style is less involved than that of Kant (who habitually said : "synthetic unity of apperception" for what Locke had called "understanding") it was not much less involved. One day he was lecturing his class upon the origin of ideas. For an hour his listeners were transported in the highest realms of thought. But as he left his lecture room, one of the undergraduates plucked at his sleeve and asked timidly : "Please, Mr. Green, where did you say our ideas come from ?".

The *Prolegomena to Ethics* sets out the foundations of metaphysics, as well as of ethics, as Green understood them. First comes the flat rejection of what seemed so natural to Locke and Hume, that the raw materials of our knowledge are the sensations that force their way in upon our consciousness whether we like it or not. For when Green looked into his own mind he could not find any such things as raw sensations. He could only find complex objects held together by *relations*. It was the relations which

seemed to Green to be the *real* element in sensation. When Green looked at the sun, he saw the qualities of roundness, whiteness and heat inextricably related ; nor could he detach the sun from its relations with every other object of sense and knowledge. Since the relations were also the work of the mind, it followed that reality was (in Green's word) *spiritual*. He quotes with approval Kant's dictum : "The understanding makes Nature."

F. H. Bradley's *Appearance and Reality* went a stage further. Bradley (1846-1924) was a Fellow of Merton College, Oxford, and published several books on philosophical subjects besides the one which established his fame. The relations which had seemed to Green the very sign and substance of Reality struck Bradley quite the other way. It was from the relations which held the world together that Bradley deduced the *unreality* of the world. He argued somewhat like this. The world is strung together like the links of a chain. Each link is connected with the next link. But what is this connection ? Either it is something, in which case it must itself be connected with the links and so on in an infinite regress ; or it is nothing, in which case the links are not connected at all. Thus whatever is related contradicts itself. There may be two opinions upon this argument ; to my mind it reads like the arguments of the sophists in the *Euthyphron*, upon which Mill was exercising his critical faculties at the age of seven or so. With this weapon in his hands, Bradley assailed all the departments of conventional knowledge. Matter was unreal because it involved relations. Space and time were unreal, pain and pleasure mere appearances, soul and body the phantasmagoria of imperfect minds. What remained ? Only the Absolute. In the Absolute all human experience (for experience, although unreal, was nevertheless the only constituent of the Absolute) fell tidily into place, having shed its relations as a butterfly sloughs off its chrysalis. Bradley's style is clipped, vigorous, as if disarming the reader's incredulity by a show of businesslike precision. His rare metaphors flicker brilliantly and impatiently through the pages. He disdains illustrations as inexact and unworthy of an adult audience. We have travelled a long way since Locke bent down to listen to the unformed babble of little children.

Mill once said that philosophy must always take one of two courses and philosophers walk in opposite ways accordingly. Either they will hold that our knowledge is built up slowly and imperfectly by experience ; or they will cleave to one or other form of the doctrine of innate ideas. This sums up the fundamental schism of the nineteenth century.

V

WE have reached the Modern Age, having proceeded, as Nature was once reputed never to do, by jumps. We have left gaps; we have suppressed many worthy names; and we have somewhat obscured that ancient truth that men who have seen the light have generally done so by climbing on another's shoulders.

How many near-great philosophers the universities have produced— great, if you take into account their influence upon their pupils and successors. Such a one was Robert Grosseteste, the first Chancellor of Oxford University, who lectured to Roger Bacon. He was an Englishman in the grand style, fearlessly outspoken, a hater of Popery, who built upon philosophy like a rock. Even Bacon writes of him with reverence. Or consider, five hundred years later, that galaxy of philosophers who won a brilliant reputation for the Scottish universities : Francis Hutcheson, professor at Glasgow, forerunner of the Utilitarians ; Thomas Reid of Aberdeen, Hume's critic and rival ; and Dugald Stewart in Edinburgh, the most quoted of J. S. Mill's authorities on logic. Hobbes made a furious attack on the universities as being stickers in the mud of reaction ; and Adam Smith, in his time, added a more gentle rebuke. Nevertheless, without the universities, British philosophy would have been poorer ; and Hobbes' assault upon the professors was the least successful of his many feuds.

When we run into the nineteenth century, the universities become even more prominent. The reason for this may be found in the increasing endowment of philosophic studies. Hutcheson has been called "the first notable British philosopher to occupy a professor's Chair"; and that was in 1729. In June 1842, that is to say, almost exactly 100 years ago, the universities of Oxford, Cambridge, Dublin, Edinburgh, Glasgow, Aberdeen, St. Andrews, London and Durham, supported between them some eighteen professorships and lectureships in pure Philosophy (excluding Divinity and Natural Philosophy). To-day the same universities can count, at a conservative estimate, more than fifty such posts. This takes no account of Professorships in Psychology and other border-line subjects. In addition, the great industrial cities have now acquired universities, each with its own Faculty of Philosophy. Birmingham has one Professorship and two Lectureships in Mental and Moral Philosophy; the Universities of Manchester, Liverpool and Leeds make very similar provision. Where knowledge was once husbanded in channels, it now flows like a river.

At the same time, more and more young people are enabled to indulge that not ignoble curiosity which prompts us to ask philosophic questions and ponder the last uncertainties. Only in a university can such unworldly pursuits be carried on communally and single-mindedly. I still recall, with mixed astonishment and delight, the smoke-filled evenings in a friend's college rooms where, with Professor G. E. Moore for company, we used to implant our eyes upon the ceiling, trying to discover whether or not we were directly acquainted with universals, whether, in other words, we could see whiteness itself or only a white expanse of plaster! I can still see Professor C. D. Broad lecturing in Trinity College, rosy, cherubic, repeating each sentence, like the wise thrush, twice (or was it three times?) over, while the more industrious of his class scribbled their notes. A continual half-smile lingered about his lips, as if he found the whole business irrepressibly comic; and once or twice during the hour he would bring the house down with a sally against M'Taggart, who had lectured at Trinity before him and taught that Time was unreal, or against Leibniz' fantastic conception of a table as a colony of unintelligent souls. I now greatly regret never having heard J. M. Keynes lecture. Keynes' subject was the same which had occupied J. S. Mill: the problem of induction and the justification of general laws. His *Treatise on Probability* is held to have superseded all former studies in this highly technical province of logic. Keynes must be claimed as the only first-rank philosopher who has become a Director of the Bank of England; he has handsomely continued the tradition of carrying philosophy into the world of affairs.

Two strong winds have blown across modern philosophy. One is the new science of psychology. This was originally a department of philosophy, springing directly from the introspective exercises of Descartes, Locke and Hume; but it developed such a practical bent in its applications to medicine and industry that its divorce from philosophy is now almost complete. The advance in psychological knowledge has modified some of the older philosophic ideas out of all recognition. It would be considered very naïve nowadays to accept Locke's "simple ideas of sensation." When we "see the sun" we have to consider a *total sense-field* out of which our faculty of *attention* selects a central object ("the sun") which we may call a *sense-datum*. Nor can our sense-datum be any longer impaled upon a point of time; it lasts through a *specious present* containing within itself a past, a present and a future. To this experience are added certain *feelings* (*e.g.*, eye-strain) as well as *conations* (*e.g.*, a desire to shut the eyes). Another new conception with which psychology has confronted the philosophers is that of the "unconscious mental processes" of which so much has been made by Freud and his school. Most philosophers have rejected the "unconscious mind" as a misinterpretation of something which requires further analysis, but the "quasi-mnemic traces" which unconsciously influence human behaviour are a fact of which our philosophy of mind must henceforward take notice.

The other major stir has been the New Physics, the Relativity Theory and the Space-Time Hypothesis, usually associated with the name of Einstein. The intense popular interest in this subject has been demonstrated by the success of such books as Sir Arthur Eddington's *Nature of the Physical World* and Mr. Dunne's *Experiment with Time*. No doubt these books fell outside the stricter confines of philosophy. Miss Susan Stebbing's stricture upon Eddington illustrates an extreme professional view. (Miss Stebbing also illustrates the important thesis that Englishwomen may qualify, not only as Members of Parliament and aircraft designers, but also as Professors of Philosophy). Some philosophers, *e.g.* Professor A. N. Whitehead, have used Space-Time as a solvent of old philosophic dilemmas like Locke's distinction between the primary and secondary qualities of objects. According to Locke (and to most of his successors) nothing can be really coloured because the colours of things vary with the standpoint of the observer and the hour of day. Whitehead attempts to show, with the help of the Einsteinian physics, that a thing can actually *be* two different colours at once by being pervaded from two different regions of Space-Time. The argument is highly technical and may not be sound, but the fact that it is attempted shows how a revolution in physics may revolutionise philosophy, as Bacon and his friends once blazed a trail for the scientists.

A happy convention exists which holds the historian excused from extending the well-established judgments of the past to living people. But it is a fair guess that of this young century's philosophers Bertrand Russell will be longest remembered. His influence has gone far beyond his native island ; his work is well known, not only in the United States of America where he has held many university appointments, but also in the schools of philosophy of India and the Far East. He has been a controversial figure as wildly admired and reprobated as Spinoza in his time. He has suffered imprisonment and exile for his ideas.

Russell has inherited an earldom from his grandfather who was a Liberal Prime Minister of England. He was also a follower of J. S. Mill. The many links with the older philosophers form perhaps the most remarkable part of Russell's story. In his *Outline of Philosophy* he acknowledges his philosophic ancestry in these words :

"I come now to the triad of British philosophers, Locke, Berkeley and Hume —English, Irish and Scotch respectively. Perhaps from patriotic bias or from community of national temperament, I find more that I can accept and regard as still important in the writings of these three than in the philosophy of their continental predecessors."

Like Locke especially, Russell has followed his chief metaphysical works with the broadest ethical and social enquiries. *On Education, Marriage and Morals, The Conquest of Happiness* show Locke's Libertarianism and Bentham's Utilitarianism carried to the extreme conclusion. Russell's ethic is a *greatest happiness principle* from which all stoical reservations have been purged away : a sort of quintessential Utilitarianism.

"We need a morality based upon love of life, upon pleasure in growth and positive achievement . . . . A man should be regarded as "good" if he is happy, expansive, generous and glad when others are happy . . . . A man who acquires a fortune by cruelty or exploitation should be regarded as at present we regard what is called an "immoral" man and he should be so regarded even if he goes to church regularly."

Russell himself recalls how he first heard the name of Bentham as that of a very wicked man ! Russell's latest published book : *An Enquiry into Meaning and Truth*, returns to the problem of language almost exactly as it was first formulated by Francis Bacon and afterwards by Locke and Mill. To Bacon's objection that Reality is too subtle for words and to Locke's objection that all language entails abstraction, Russell envisages a primary logical language which shall copy the fundamental operations of nature. Russell matches the best of his predecessors with a beautifully direct style, capable of savage irony and elegant wit. I have always liked the riposte to the Behaviourist philosopher who found something incongruous in Keynes' marrying a famous dancer. This, said Russell, was from the Behaviourist standpoint most unreasonable (for the Behaviourists contend that all thinking is nothing more than a muscular agitation in the throat). She had cultivated the muscles of legs and arms, he the muscles of the larynx, so that both were acrobats, though belonging to different branches of the profession !

No absolutely consistent account of the universe emerges from Russell's many writings. He has undoubtedly changed his point of view more than once. There was an early period when he was much attracted to Idealism. He tells us himself that he was once very much under the spell of Bradley's *Appearance and Reality*. In one early book he even suggests a revival of the Platonic Overworld of Ideas, in which universals exist timelessly, diffusing reality upon particular things. But Russell, too, felt the impact of the new physical theories. It was necessary to re-examine the question, "What is a physical object?" and re-define the evasive relation of Matter and Mind. He returned once more to the

BERTRAND RUSSELL b. 1872
Drawing by Sir William Rothenstein

analysis of the sense-field or sense-datum, the original Lockian "idea of sensation." He found there a hard neutral core, divested of all accompanying feelings—a core which partook of the nature of neither matter nor mind. This neutral stuff, according to Russell, was the elemental stuff of which the universe was made ; in certain combinations it was called mind, in other combinations it became a physical object. The sense-datum which was *perceived* formed part of a mind and a physical object simultaneously, just as some Thames-side towns belong to Berkshire in the postal sense and to Buckinghamshire topographically. It is easier to reconstruct the physical world on this basis than to explain the extraordinary variety of "events" (as Russell sometimes calls them) which constitute a self or mind. As far as I know, Russell has nowhere indicated how such a task would be accomplished. But if it were, both minds and physical objects would become, for philosophers, logical constructions built upon elements which were immediately known. It is an arresting theory and one which may be worked out in detail by a later generation.

We are also confirmed in the belief, as we read Russell and other modern philosophers, that the perennial task of philosophy is to re-state and re-define truths which have been stated and defined, but imperfectly, in the past. Sometimes an old term is discarded for no better reason than that it does not sound fresh and will not serve what is essentially a fresh effort of thought. It is ironical, for instance, that Russell should abandon the word "knowledge" for the word "acquaintance"; we no longer know what we see, we are only acquainted with it! The "innate idea" of Locke's predecessors has become "the a priori judgment"; the "Platonic idea" is renamed "universal." Philosophy, like political liberty, is not to be entrapped in any written constitution; it has to be struggled for, by each succeeding age, with new angles of view and new forms of expression. That is why we should read the history of philosophy imaginatively and why we should deal gently with the outworn terminologies of the past. For our own most cherished exactitudes, our "basic propositions" and "perceptual situations" and "emergent characteristics" will be ruthlessly spring-cleaned by our children and grandchildren, who will often wonder why on earth we expressed ourselves as we did.

Is there any connection between a nation's philosophy and its other activities, its foreign policies, its social and economic organisation? That depends on whether its men of action are willing to become philosophers and if its philosophers are willing to be political handicraftsmen. More than two thousand years ago Plato prophesied that there would be no good government in the world until philosophers became kings. And if this is interpreted as an allegory, we may suppose that Plato had it in mind to define human perfection as a sort of marriage between high thought and virtuous action: which must be for ever the aim of man. If we measure our British philosophers against this standard, they may fall short, but not so far as we might have expected.